WITH THE OFFAL EATERS

To surprise you pleasantly and try to get you thir
than I thought it would so far!'

Because most importantly ... "Step 1" of a safety talk is, as below, to "Introduce yourself, break the ice and set the right tone" and I've tried in my own fashion to 'model' that here.

I'd like to tell you a third story that illustrates perfectly the sort of dedication I so often see in the safety community and the obstacles it faces. I attended a key kick-off meeting with a safety professional who didn't seem his usual enthusiastic self. I'll call him Ian Steel. As we chatted away waiting for the board to join us (they were late) he explained that he was having a bad day. A very bad day actually as he explained that he'd buried his father that morning. I was staggered and asked "What on earth are you doing *here*?" but he simply said "I know... but this session is *really* important".

I found this very humbling and it reminded me that whilst the **devil** can certainly be in the detail of a simple conversation or act – so too can **inspiration**. The late great inspirational safety speaker Ian Whittingham MBE used to describe the aftermath of his accident to remind us that events ripple out like dropping a stone in a pond. This works for positive events too. When I feel I'm banging my head against the wall of 'impressive words, less impressive action' I think of Ian Steel and the others like him I've met. Every good safety conversation sends out good ripples and is a brick in the wall of a strong safety culture.

I hope you find the book useful.

Tim Marsh
October, 2011

"Talking Safety"

A User's Guide to a World Class Safety Conversation

By Dr Tim Marsh

Dedication
For my Mother and Father

Acknowledgement
I am again enormously grateful to Prof Neil Budworth former President of IOSH whose constructive comments and suggestions were, as ever, hugely helpful.

Published by Ryder-Marsh (Safety) Ltd.

Introduction.

This booklet is in part intended as a concise companion for the longer, original "Affective Safety Management" book but is also a stand alone for the reader whose view is:-

"145 reasonably concise pages with a few nice cartoons is all very well but could you produce something that is more concise and tells me exactly what to do for "a first step"? Minimum theory, maximum "80:20" principle, no options or alternatives, just what to do for the first step... what do we do if we don't do anything else?"

The good news is that, as ever, the 80:20 principle applies and if you only do this 'step one' at all well you'll achieve the fabled step change of a 50% reduction in accidents with this alone. I absolutely *guarantee* it.

There has to be a little theory for background I'm afraid - no-one will do anything if you don't explain "why" as well as "what" nor will they adapt well to unusual circumstances - but I've aimed to keep that as concise as possible.

Two Stories by Way of Introduction

If you'll allow me a little indulgence before the off I'd like to start with two stories to introduce myself and the booklet. Both *entirely* true.

The first refers to a Welsh rugby legend, Bobby Windsor, who was a neighbour of mine in South Wales. Indeed my father, who was a teacher, taught him at school. Bobby was part of the famous Pontypool front row - the "Viet-Gwent" - and toured South Africa successfully in 1974 with the British Lions achieving a famous series win!

In those days there were no mobile phones, of course, and a team meeting was called to sort out the problem of someone continually sneaking into the management's rooms to make phone calls home.

The management got the squad together and offered the offender the chance to confess.

Nothing.

They pointed out that all the calls were to the same number and that it was a *Pontypool* number...

INTRODUCTION

At which Bobby leapt to his feet and shouted. "Right! Which one of you bastards has been phoning my wife!?"

The Moral - There are times when you've taken a risk when you'll need to think on your feet.

Story 2. My Aunty Shirley was pulled over for speeding by a young PC. He asked to see her driving licence but she said she didn't have one.

He asked if it was her car even but she said "No it belonged to a Tom Jukes". She was asked if Mr Jukes had lent her the car and she said that no she'd stolen it but only after she'd killed Tom, chopped him up and put him in the boot.

Shaken, the young PC called for back up and presently a senior officer arrived and took charge of the situation. "Please step to the boot and open it Madam" he asked. My Aunt did so. The boot was empty.

"Interesting..." he opined and asked "Could I see your drivers licence please?" and she said "certainly" and handed it over. "Is this your car?" he asked. "Yes officer. Would you like to see the log book?" she smiled.

"No need for that" said the officer continuing "but this is really very interesting. My young officer over there told me that you don't have a driving licence and that this isn't your car. Indeed he says that you stole this car from a Mr Tom Jukes after you killed him, chopped him up and put him in the boot here".

My Auntie's response: ... "Oh the lying little bugger! I bet he's only gone and told you I was *speeding* as well!"

The Moral – As above, if you are going to take risks at least keep your wits about you.

And Your Point Is?! You May Ask...

You may be thinking that these two so called 'learning points' can't possibly underpin a safety book and you'd be right of course. As ever with a psychologist you just can't trust them and there's a hidden agenda.

What I've tried to do here is the following three things:-

To amuse you. (Simply because if you're smiling that's a good thing in itself. Life is too short is it not?). But also:-

Contents.

Holiday Inn

*Proud to be the Official Hotel
Provider to the London 2012
Olympic and Paralympic Games*

Chapter One - Some Theory

It's said "You get the safety levels Senior Management want – all else is just detail and case study". For example, one of our clients is considered very much the H&S leader in their field. This stems not from any work we've done with them lately but from an incident at a funeral some 11 years ago when they were very average in terms of safety standards. An employee had been killed and at the funeral a rather apprehensive MD was approached by the widow who instead of attacking or abusing him thanked him sincerely for showing her husband the respect of attending. Relieved and humbled he made himself a promise ...

That's a *case study* and to add a little *detail* there are five strands that under-pin the approach advocated in this book. I'll try and describe how the management "Walk and Talk" is the key on-going methodology that addresses *all* of them.

The first is an assumption that the company in question has broadly reached compliance in its systems and procedures. It has good training, robust induction and risk assessment processes, for example, and up to date safety management systems. However, like all companies, what it says in the file and what happens in practise are not always the same and the "holes in the system" need investigating and plugging. This is particularly so given most companies' constant need to change and update so there will always be "new holes following changes" to sort out. Therefore, as well as the pro-active focus described below, the conversation and analysis needs constantly to loop back to the basics.

The second is based on the well known 'spot the gorilla' amidst the confusing basketball players clip. The point of this famous exercise is that if you walk the site looking *only* for safety issues you'll see 10 times as much as if you look for safety issues whilst going about your day job. Though you can of course address environmental and health issues at the same time it's generally felt that much less than two half hour walks a week isn't enough. Though everything including profit and economic viability interlink and overlap of course a conversation that is primarily 'welfare' focused is key even if it's to the planet's welfare.

The third is what is known as 'transformational leadership' which is basically where we go beyond basic training and compliance and inspire by leading by example, praising, coaching and involving the workforce in decision making and design. All the research shows, unsurprisingly, that what is led this way is what you get. The well known analogy is that pulling string is easy... pushing it next to impossible. To a great extent it's through these behaviours that we let the workforce know "what we want, what we really, really want".

The fourth strand is the Elvis 'walk a mile in a man's shoes' rule crossed with Reason's "Just Culture" model. Basically, that the value for money we get for our investments in safety improvement is limited by how well we *genuinely* understand why someone has done what they have done. Have you ever seen a 'back to floor' style programme where the person involved didn't end up saying "ah, *now* I know what I need to do" Indeed in the latest version of the programme "Undercover Boss" I made a point of counting how many bosses claimed to have learnt a huge amount. It was *all* of them and as if to illustrate the inspirational part of leadership a good fifty percent of employees actually burst into tears of gratitude when told how useful they had been ...

Therefore the fifth and final rule is what is known as the "Nike Rule" (I.E, just do it! Though personally I prefer what's known as the "rude Nike"). This rule relates directly to management commitment. We don't get what we say we want we get what our behaviours demonstrate we really want. No magic bullets. The "Nike" always seems to apply after a funeral – but it doesn't have to be that way. We can move forward a lot from just a little effort sometimes – but effort there always has to be.

The basic "Walk and Talk" model detailed here seeks to ensure we've got the above covered if only under the "80:20" banner. I hope you'll agree its all "common sense", would deliver excellent results and though very possible will be difficult at times. Frankly, if you don't think those three things by the end of the book then I've not done my job very well!

1.1 The Vital Importance of *Behaviour*

The first question to address in some detail is "Why should line management walk about the organisation talking about day to day safety *behaviour* at all"? After all most times nothing happens as a consequence.

There are several good reasons:-

First, as above, to give a practical demonstration that safety is indeed as important as it's claimed to be in the values statements and visions that a company has. To show "visible felt leadership" as it is sometimes known. We will get what we show we're most interested in is true. An active "walk and talk" process is a key element – maybe *the* key element – of showing we really do mean phrases like "If you can't do it safely don't do it at all". Obviously, most of this book is about what a good safety walk covers and what it should look and feel like.

The second reason is that there is always a direct link between the number of unsafe acts and the number of accidents. Heinrich's original famous triangle suggested that there are on average 300 unsafe acts per accident and the most recent HSE figures suggest 2M unsafe behaviours per fatality. I'd suggest arguing over the *exact* ratio doesn't matter though – because there always will be one.

It's worth acknowledging however that the ratios do vary of course depending on the behaviours and the potential outcomes. Some behaviours are frequent and reasonably trivial (though note that even trips on flat surfaces cause dozens of fatalities every year). Others are less frequent but more likely to cause fatalities – a steeper Triangle if you like. This, of course, is especially true when we look at process safety issues.

It's important to stress that the two things aren't separate, rather they interlink and overlap. A good example of this would be the housekeeping on Piper Alpha which was notoriously poor. Any meaningful analysis of the poor housekeeping would have taken the auditor to the permit to work system. Permits of the platform contained a "housekeeping put right?" element which would have demonstrated clearly a tick box mentality lacking control. Among many others this was perhaps the key factor in the explosion. Clearly, this would have been a very useful issue to have addressed in early 1996.

Therefore, although the conversation we discuss here can never take the place of systems, monitoring and auditing it certainly should *complement* them.

Simple Statistics

However, we'll always need to address day to day behaviours for their own sake. For example, if the true likelihood of falling down the stairs of a building is 100,000 to 1 but 1M people use the stairs annually – with no-one holding the handrail – then you'll have 10 accidents a year give or take. If 90%, comply then 1 accident a year give or take - but if we can get 99% to comply then only 1 accident every ten years or so. (And "zero accidents" becomes a possibility. Indeed for most companies the majority of accidents will be the result of simple slips trips, falls and "struck bys" so though process safety is of course vital to ensure something catastrophic doesn't happen - it's virtually impossible to have world class safety figures without a behavioural approach).

Heinrich and Gravity.

This is partly because the majority of accidents have gravity as the root cause and however sophisticated our systems, organisation or even country, we can't design out gravity if we want to move our product or our people.

Even call centre employees have to drive to work and climb stairs and for many utility companies the single biggest cause of accidents is retail staff tripping over in the street walking from house to house and trying to update their palmtops as they go.

Setting the Tone - Behaviour and Peer Pressure.

The third reason is that the best definition of safety culture is "the way we typically do things around here". As in all walks of life a handful of key behaviours will set the tone and the first thing we do in a new situation is to look about and "check out what's what". If we see half the 'regulars' acting safely and half unsafely then as a new start or sub contractor we can do pretty much what we want and not stand out. However, if we can get these key behaviours up over the fabled "tipping point" of 90% or so then it becomes self-sustaining.

These key behaviours will range from simple 'hold the handrail', 'look where you're walking' and PPE as above through to the quality of a tool box talk.
Indeed the latest studies suggest that 80% of what we learn is from our peers – only 5% from formal training. Imagine arriving in a new country and being told by the hire car people "we're brutal with speeding on this island ... don't even think about exceeding 100kph" reinforced with huge threatening signs as you drive out of the airport. You'd very probably join the motorway at 95kph? But you find in practise the inside lane is averaging 100, the middle 120 and the outside lane is a complete free for all. What speed would you be doing 5 minutes later? Since many will justify this with the answer "well you have to keep up with the flow!" a better question "how many of you would be in the outside lane within the hour?" (At conferences the average response to the second question is 40 to 50%. I'll return to the significance of this "40%" later when discussing the importance of designing out temptation).

Vision statements and company values are vital of course in setting the tone but they are 'necessary but not *sufficient*'. They (should!) certainly *influence* the culture but they are not *it*. The day-to-day behaviour is.

1.2 OK Day-to Day Behaviour is Vital - So Don't People Just Need to Comply and Have a "Good Attitude"?

Unfortunately *no-one* has a bad attitude. Studies show that 50% of us think we have a good attitude and 50% an average attitude (I exaggerate but only a little – the actual figures are usually about 48% & 49%). So when we say "you know who you are!" the entire audience points to the person next to them saying "they're talking about **you**". I mean have you ever won a pub argument about sport, politics or religion? Ever? Have you changed an attitude about any of those subjects in the last 20 years?

Inspirational speakers can help in the short term just as new football managers can induce a sudden boost in performance. But this honeymoon period doesn't last and soon enough we are back to the old levels of performance – unless we *change* something. (In football terms it might be cleverly re-organising the team, better organisation at set pieces or improving fitness levels). In safety terms we need to change the working environment. Or else the maxim "If you do what you always did, you get what you always got" soon applies.

Compliance and Safety

A very interesting finding is that basic compliance isn't enough anyway. Research suggests that there is a **better correlation between workforce involvement in safety and incident rate** and **compliance and incident rate.** If that sounds intuitively unlikely please consider this question. Would you prefer your 10 year old to simply step into the road blindly at a level crossing because the green 'walk' sign has come on or would you prefer them to cross 50 yards down the road but 'dynamic risk assessing' properly as they go?

1.3 Safety Involvement and Leadership

Picture an office scene from the sitcom "The Office". Not David Bent but instead "Gareth" the slightly weird looking chap who's the closest thing on the show to a front line supervisor. Picture if you can the emotional response of the 'nice one' who sits opposite.

Can you imagine this reaction if this dubious 'Gareth' chap was tasked with leading any sort of safety project or programme? Can I suggest that the likelihood of any sort of success would be zero ... because the very *best* response he'd get from his colleagues would be total apathy?

I'm sure most readers would instinctively agree with that and I'd like to spend some time describing the very well researched psychology that underpins this instinct. We are simply not going to get very far with our safety culture if our safety leaders inspire animosity rather than respect.

In the US they talk about "discretionary behaviour" and it's suggested that without it an organisation simply **cannot** develop a strong safety culture as they will never get beyond "compliant". In the UK we might refer to these as behaviours as "above the line behaviour" or "organisational citizenship behaviours".

Regardless, we are talking about behaviours like:-

• Volunteering to be part of a project or process team or to be a safety rep.
• Undertaking non-mandatory safety training or attending non-mandatory meetings
• Paying any sort of genuine attention or contributing to a discussion during *mandatory* training or meetings!
• Saying something to a colleague who has put themselves at risk
• Making an effort to model safe behaviours and practises in front of new starts
• Taking the time to show new starts the ropes
• Stopping to clear a housekeeping issue
• Stopping to call a "time out" because you're not comfortable
• Reporting a near miss
• Responding (totally!) honestly to questions during an incident investigation

And so on.

For what it's worth how many organisations that have all the systems, training and procedures in place to have acquired any number of compliance certificates on reception walls are anywhere near as *genuinely compliant* on a daily basis as they'd like to be? So to deliberately blur the edges between compliance and "discretionary behaviour" we could describe discretionary behaviour as:-

• Complying with a safety requirement when not supervised or working alone.

Because, let's be honest, often what should be compliance is actually discretionary – especially if it's late or you're working from a van a long way from base.

But regardless of blurred edges I hope that we'd all agree that the above list is simply the basic behaviours we'd **all** like to see our workforce undertaking. It's what we want when we get inspirational speakers in, set up behavioural safety processes, or launch "hearts and minds" initiatives. Again, this is important as the research suggests that we simply **can't have them** in any widespread or enduring way in the absence of what has been described as "transformational leadership".

Aubrey Daniels makes the point that management and leadership are different things with leaders by definition needing followers. He also stresses that any successful leader will have *willing* followers. An Australian paper asks more directly "what sort of effing supervisor are you anyway!?" Boiled down this Australian paper describes three types of leader –

• the fireman;
• the policeman and
• the knight.

The "fireman" is "reactive" of course – invisible until something goes wrong. The "policeman" is primarily about actively seeking out transgressions and ensuring basic compliance.

We need our front line leaders to be the third sort, pro-active "knights". Supervisors leading from the front with passion, honour and integrity!

Certainly, to avoid the fate of Gareth from the office we need to be somewhere near a baseline of a fair and just policeman as a minimum. Someone the workforce trusts and respects enough not to dismiss out of hand? As in "They're not really my cup of tea but they're solid enough I suppose – you know where you are" in smoke shack speak.

Can we perhaps just call it "being the sort of leader you'd entrust your children with"?

What Does 'Transformational' Leadership Look Like?

Traditionally 'Transformational Leadership' is held to have 4 key elements:-

• Listening
• Rewarding
• Leading by Example
• Involving

Importantly, you'll see that following the five step model outlined in this booklet *explicitly* covers these four issues. (Although broadly speaking leaders should of course apply them at all times to all things of course). This book also makes the case that really good safety leadership will also have "learning" included and in safety terms this adds the principles and tools of Just Culture to Transformational Leadership.

1.4 "Mindful" Leadership – A Check-Sheet of Issues Worth Considering

The highly influential Australian writer Andrew Hopkins has studied the causes of major accidents all over the world and insists that organisations must be 'mindful' if they are to have strong safety culture.

It's a (final – I promise!) concept that pulls together many of the threads discussed above and gives us a first check-sheet to consider.

This mindfulness of course must come from the top and he says bluntly that "leaders set the tone and managers have to live with that". He's being simplistic of course as it's the supervisors who set the tone day to day – though to a great extent always taking their cue from senior management. (He says himself that's just a provocative comment to start a debate – but we all understand what he means and broadly agree I'd expect).

The mindfulness notion is in complete accord with the other most influential writers on the subject whether we are considering James Reason's concept of a 'vulnerable' organisation or Scott Geller's 'Total Safety Culture' where he stresses safety can't be a priority ('priorities change daily and are political') it must be a core value, embedded in the very DNA of the company so that's it very much "what we do around here". In short, it's a version of Aubrey Daniels' assertion that "we get the safety standards that senior management want – no more, no less".

He stresses that good safety leadership will involve the loss of sleep to the thought "how do I know XYZ wont happen?" and is analogous to the core DuPont philosophy that if you're not actively pushing forwards you're almost certainly drifting backwards.

The intention of this book is to utilise the 80:20 principle to give managers practical tools that will allow any organisation to positively address the key elements of these principles. Below is a list of a number of issues that are worth looking at when undertaking a 'mindful' 'walk and talk'.

The very basics:-

• Has the organisation ensured people know who is responsible for the various safety tasks or do "two people think they are so no one actually is"

• Are tool box talks and weekly briefs clear, user-friendly and with understanding confirmed (not just knocked off with a "sign here it's your signature I need and I'm not too bothered if you don't even speak English").

• Do risk assessments involve genuine reflection and objective thought - or are they more photocopy, sign, file.

• Do meetings start with "safety number one on the agenda" but with everyone aware that's to "get it out of the way before cracking on with the important stuff?"

• Consider the organisational structure. Is it easy to communicate concerns upwards or totally impossible (as, for example, you'd need to go through the person you're concerned about even though you know for a fact they are not going to see this as a learning opportunity!)

• Are the people responsible for writing systems and procedures empowered to ensure they are actually followed?

• Do the people who write the systems and procedures actively consult the end users as a systematic part of the design process?

• Is maintenance work reactive with machinery run to fail rather than pro-active?

More 'mindful' issues

• Ask someone a production or quality related question. Check the speed of the response, the facts they have at their disposal and how keen they appear to reassure you they have everything under control. Then ask them a safety related question of similar type.

- Look out for the use of the word "but" which in a middle of a sentence basically means "ignore what I've just said. The important stuff is coming up" so "do it safely but do it by Friday" meaning something very different from "do it by Friday but do it safely".

- Sit in on a formal appraisal without mentioning your interest is primarily in safety. Monitor the body language of the appraiser and the appraised. Is it as intense when talking about safety items as when talking about productivity? (Or does this look like the pre-match/ half time warm up rather than the real thing?)

- Consider when the last time the person you're talking to worried about a safety issue pro-actively rather than reactively.

- Consider whether "good news audits" produce an automatic sceptical response (lots of infamous incidents were preceded by a string of positive audits – for example Piper Alpha). Hopkins suggests "a string of continuous good news – that should set alarm bells ringing"

- Consider how senior management respond to bad news. Do they even *look* inconvenienced even though assuring through clenched teeth that they aren't? (I once asked an MD at a board meeting if he ever responded negatively to a safety issue being raised and he was adamant "never!" I asked "not even with the eyes?" and the whole room burst into laughter as I was notorious for this. Luckily he wasn't a defensive man – laughed at himself and we were off ...)

- Has someone raised a safety issue that was basically ignored? (A characteristic of nearly all major incidents)

- If an incident is mentioned in conversation it's worth following it up by tracking it through the reporting system. How far did it get? What was learned? What was the done with this learning? Even the best companies with highly expensive tracking systems will often find that the answers to these questions are concerning.

- When looking at the analysis that flows from incidents imagine you have a big red "curious why" stamp. Do any points noted beg asking the "but why did that happen? question?" If so the investigation probably hasn't gone deeply enough and you're targeting a symptom not a root cause.

- Pro-actively look at the trends in the reporting system. Are there divisions, shifts or other demographics that are hardly ever reported? If so then dig into it and find out what the blockages are and why.

Finally has there been any cost cutting recently – or maybe a "renegotiated" contract? If so was it risk assessed really thoroughly for the "law of unintended consequences" or were assumptions made that all will be well? With that law in mind it's always worth checking who is being rewarded for what. Some examples:-

• The number of "walk and talks" is monitored but not the quality so you get targets met by a flurry of crap ones at the end of the month.

• Procurement are rewarded for cutting costs but no one checks if any false economies result as a consequence (For example, cheaper PPE that no-one actually wears as it's uncomfortable or isn't fit for purpose; cheap components that fail and leak; manpower cuts that mean there is genuinely no time to check or to think and plan).

• Bonuses that are paid only on lost time incidents so management focus on these and not on process safety issues (as at Texas City).

And last but most certainly not least:-

• The way contractors are remunerated and selected. (Because as you well know the term "a whole can of worms" was coined with this in mind specifically!)

It's not an exhaustive list of course but it should give anyone plenty to be mindful of!

1.5 Toilet Bowls in Amsterdam – Nudge Theory

If you've heard of nudge theory you'll know the most famous example is the well placed ceramic fly on the toilet bowl that men can't help but point at – reducing splashing and associated cleaning costs by a full 50% apparently. (But seriously, just try and match that with a rule, extra supervision or a training programme!)

It's hugely influential at the moment with examples including empty police vans parked up near potential trouble spots, tax forms asking "are you sure you didn't forget anything?" and motorway signs saying "don't litter other people don't!" (This is a nudge with reference to social norms for what it's worth).

I've listed a lot of unintended nudges above that throw a large shadow and in a later chapter we'll discuss how failing to lead by example has huge consequences but some more pro-active companies are already trying to use 'nudge' theory to advantage. Shell Scandinavia, for example, has stopped asking platforms "why did you shut down?" and instead ask "why did you think it safe to start back up?" You'll note that the *technical* element of the answer is exactly the same – but the shadow it throws is entirely different though.

1.6 Safety is Not An Academic Exercise its a "Guerrilla War"

Reason's cheese model shows that the more weaknesses there are from strategic management decisions, through supervision and process safety to individual actions, then the more likely the holes in the slices of 'Swiss Cheese' are to line up and an accident occur. This model shows that with the benefit of hindsight *all* accidents could have been prevented and of course influences the various "target zero" campaigns.

I once gave a talk to a shipbuilder about this model whose senior management approached me afterwards to observe "we should never have agreed to build these ships this way". I used to tell conference audience about that comment and leave it at that. However, Reason's most recent work on "knot in the rubber band" theory moves away from this and suggests why target zero can be so controversial.

He says that once we start work in the modern world all sorts of pressures will automatically try to stretch the rubber band away from goodness – such as sub contractors, time pressures, unexpected delays etc. The key is to not ever get overstretched so that the knot moves beyond a genuine productivity/ safety balance (as in a balanced scorecard perhaps) and becomes 'overstretched' so that the company is 'vulnerable'. When we are vulnerable an incident is overly likely and of-course the HSE will take a dim view if the company is seen in hindsight to have been overstretched and "an accident waiting to happen".

In the real world, says this model, *somebody* was going to agree to build the ships that way and that pockets of vulnerability will *inevitably* pop up from time to time and from place to place even if the overall culture is strong and the planning thorough. The trick then is to be geared to spot them quickly, and respond to them effectively so that balance is quickly restored. This is entirely analogous to the key principles of HSG 48 which looks at Human Error and says:-

• Design the job so that error is unlikely
• Make sure you have mechanisms in place to spot it when it (inevitably) happens
• Make sure you can respond quickly when it happens.

Following from this safety is then best thought of as an on-going guerrilla war and like any such war we can't win entirely in the long run but we can delay the inevitable almost indefinitely. To do this we'll need keen intelligence and data and to cleverly use the resources at our disposal.

Some managers I've spoken to report that though they of course wholly buy into a 'target zero' *concept* the day-to-day reality can seem daunting – even inducing a little fatalistic thinking at times. However, I've not met a management team that didn't feel they could buy into the 'don't overstretch the rubber band/ guerrilla war' mindset.

This book is, of-course, intended as a 'How to fight the safety guerrilla war handbook!'

Conclusion

The best organisations are truly mindful of safety in their very DNA and the very best way of demonstrating and delivering this is management walking the floor to demonstrate a genuine commitment to safety. This is achieved by frequent and high quality interactions with the workforce specifically about behavioural and other safety issues.

- Just talking about safety.
- Asking the right questions and knowing what to look for
- Debating safety issues.
- Analysing safety issues.
- Praising good safety when they see it.
- Coaching safety when they can.
- And sometimes laying the law down when that's appropriate.

The rest of the booklet tries to define what "well" looks like.

Section 2 – The "Walk and Talk" Safety Contact.

Walk and Talk - Overview.

We felt that the safety contact needs five simple but distinct phases. Actually, to be more specific it needs an appropriate combination of the following 5 phases and one of the aims of this book is to provide the reader with some tools to help them decide what "appropriate" means in each individual situation.

1 Introduce Yourself, Break the Ice and Set the Tone
2 Analysis
3 Coaching
4 Eliciting a Promise?
5 Closing Out

Walk and Talk and Workforce Behavioural Safety.

This booklet isn't about behavioural safety directly, but just for the record, the overlap here is primarily with the second step – analysis. Ideally, a company will, in time, introduce a behavioural programme that involves the workforce directly in the on-going analysis of unsafe behaviour. Possibly this will be through limited time duration project teams – or some form of on-going peer to peer observation *process* (if the latter, then measurement and feedback charts might come into play too as well as locally tailored awareness raising sessions ... and so on).

I hope that the reader will see that a good 'walk and talk' process is an excellent way to start to meaningfully address behavioural issues. As stated earlier in the book, "if you're going to do just one thing, do this".

Suggested Frequency of Safety Contacts.

Aubrey Daniels stresses that there are three levels of learning. There's basic learning, then mastery of the basics – then, finally **fluency**. Mastery is "I can now do it with a degree of confidence" and tends to be achieved after 30 or so practises. (Imagine learning to play golf or work as a volunteer on the Samaritan's helpline - or any other skill of that type. When would you stop saying "Sometimes I get it right but I'm still learning to" and start saying "I am a...")

Fluency, however, is where these skills are embedded to the extent that our driving skills are after a time. I like to think I'm a reasonably fluent speaker at conferences these days – but it took a few years and I'm certainly better now than I was once I'd done my 30 and had become broadly competent ...

This notion of fluency is analogous to the other leading US safety writer Scott Geller who says that safety must be something truly embedded not as a priority (they change and are political but as a core value "part of the DNA". "Our culture is what we do around here... automatically").

A core value is well illustrated by the sailor famous for turning back and rescuing a fellow around the world competitor in the Arctic. His well received inspirational talk builds to a simple question from the audience which is "how long did it take you to abandon the months-long race and turn back when you realised it had to be you?" His answer "Oh 4 or 5 seconds... it's the values of the sea... I didn't even need to think about it" (His challenge is "can you match that with your safety statements?" and from the shuffling in the audience it was clear not many felt they could).

Therefore, a simple point: What do you imagine we think when companies tell us they have management's commitment to undertake at least 1 or 2 safety contacts a year! Even doing one a month means it will take you around 3 years to reach basic mastery. So I'd like to suggest that one a month is an absolute *minimum*!

This is also important for another reason. If our trainees do not go out and use the behaviours we've requested on training courses how can we give them feedback and embed these behaviours?

Embedding Training.

Basic motivation theory explains why so many training courses are a waste of money. To be effective, training first needs to explain *what* we want people to do and be clear who needs to do it (as in "if two people think they're responsible then no one is"). However, we also need to take the trouble to explain *why* – or the average worker will feel slighted and be apt to drag their heels. We then need to address "how" to do what we want them to do because if an employee is worried that they can't do something competently they'll often find any excuse not to do it at all in case they make a fool of themselves.

Finally, we need to consider whether the individual values the outcome. Importantly we need to think of this combination of *what & why*, *how* and *valued* as not something we stack on top of each other but rather as something we multiply - so a low score *anywhere* means a low score overall.

Therefore it's vital that the typical front line supervisor really needs to be taught to value the outcome by the organisation. An experienced safety professional of my acquaintance would summarise it thus. "If the behaviours requested are not considered career enhancing in the smoke shack 6 months after the training course then they won't be happening and you'll have wasted your money".

We achieve this through *formal* and *informal* feedback. Formal feedback would be giving safety items prominence in the appraisal. As we discussed in the first section some companies don't have them in there at all or give them only perfunctory coverage on the day. (By which I mean both the appraiser and the person being appraised clearly relax a little through these items whilst collecting their thoughts before getting back to something more important!) Informal feedback can be summarised with our own adaptation of Aubrey Daniels "tick" rating. A worker observed acting safely? - a tick! A supervisor praising a worker for acting safely two ticks! A manager praising a supervisor for praising a worker acting safely – three ticks!

I'm sure you get the idea ... the reverse would be a manager seeing a supervisor fail to challenge an unsafe act (as requested on a recent course) and saying nothing. No ticks for anyone. And no behaviour change at all likely either.

In short we need to:-

• Train our managers and supervisors in what to do
• Explain why they need to do it
• Give them the skills and tools to ensure they can do them well
• Ensure they do them often enough to master the basics

and

• Give them feedback to ensure they refine and embed these behaviours

2.1 Introduce Yourself and Set the Tone.

First Something Hugely Important – Modelling (Or "don't be the "T*t with the Toupe").

A key thing you *must always do* is to model safety at all times yourself. (Whether undertaking a safety conversation or not).

My first book (ASM) has an illustrative Gordon Brown story which in short involved him declining to wear eye protection during a site visit and management letting him get away with it because of the inconvenience of refusing to walk him about. The CEO still says "I've paid for that decision every day since. The lads didn't say as we hoped 'I'd have done the same if I'd been in Vick's shoes' … they leapt on it with glee and every tool box talk and briefing and *especially* at any disciplinary we get 'what about Gordon Brown!?'. If I could turn the clock back I would!"

I've since had an experience that you might find amusing.

One of our clients had a visit from a senior chap from HQ who flatly refused to don his hard hat during a site visit. Quickly the local secretaries spoke to their contacts at HQ and found out that it was because he wore a wig and was worried it would come off and embarrass him. As well as causing our PPE enhancement process no end of problems for months you might be amused to know that even before he'd even left site he was know as the "tit with the toupe". (That's the cleaned up version – the actual alliteration was on the letter "w" – as in wig). So as well as everything else the 'maintaining dignity' plan not working quite the way he'd intended then!

So rule one is always follow the rules yourself.

Setting the Tone

I tried to make a start on this section in the introduction with my Aunty Shirley and Bobby Windsor stories. Whilst we're certainly not advocating you start your talk with a few gags and funny stories we *are* advocating that you don't plough straight in to the analytical elements.

Instead take the time to chat to the person a bit starting with a brief introduction of who you are and what you're doing. You could ask:-

• How are you?

• What's it like doing your job nowadays?

• What are the safety implications (you might want to refer to any risk assessment).

Talk about the weekend's sporting events perhaps but just get them *talking* and at their ease. Time invested here in doing this will pay dividends later when you get to the meat of the conversation.

Building Trust

Indeed, studies show that admitting you don't know everything and asking questions increases a person's level of trust in you rather then reducing their respect. Therefore, since enhancing trust is something we are *all* aiming for within companies, asking questions and listening to the answer is a key component of a good safety talk – or any other talk for that matter.

Perhaps the best known safety culture model is that of the "Bradley Curve" which suggests that we need to move from dependent ("I'll act safely if you're watching") through "independent" ("I'll act safely even on my own") to, finally "interdependent" where we are each our brother's keeper. As you can imagine *trust* is a hugely important element of this most advanced element - interdependence.

Some Do's and Don'ts

Obviously the first don't is that whilst it will never be entirely convenient it's best not to stop someone when it's extremely inconvenient or even dangerous!

A second don't is to never finish the sentence for them. It's worth stressing again that it's vital that you *listen* even if you know the answers already. It's getting them comfortable talking to you that's key here.

Also never ask closed questions if you can avoid it – you'll often get closed answers in response. (Closed questions can be answered with a simple "yes" or "no" – open questions ask for example "what do you think?") People will of course say "yes" or "no" if they can whether or not that's true just to get rid of you as quickly as possible even when they have something useful to say. (You'll have been stopped by a market research person I'm sure and tried to get away but if they can stop you and get you talking then often you'll be saying "and write this down too!" long after their eyes have glazed over and they've got what they needed ... or perhaps that's just me!)

What you **mustn't** do is to get too "matey" and step beyond friendly and human and into unprofessional. It might make the session pass nicely for you but you won't have the impact you want by being "one of the guys".

Setting the Tone Summary:-

* *Always* lead by example
* Remember that whilst there will never be an ideal time and location – some times and locations are better than others!
* Be friendly and personable but not overly 'matey'
* Remember that admitting you don't know everything makes you more trusted
* Use open questions to get them talking
* Listen

2.2 Analysis

The second stage of the conversation is the analysis of any issues raised and this is where the principles of 'Just Culture' come into play. 'Just Culture' is a model that takes the overly simplistic "no name, no blame" approach forward by stressing that if we analyse objectively we'll find that the majority of unsafe acts are for a reason that makes, at least, a certain sense if you genuinely understand the root cause. Only in the minority of cases will a person be off on a folly of their own. The key thing here is to be as *analytical* and *learning* focused as possible as whatever happens next will be limited by the accuracy of your analysis.

This is worth stating really bluntly. If you have £100 to spend on safety and 80% of the causes of unsafe acts are physical or cultural and only 20% are individual - you need to spend £80 on changing the physical and cultural issues and only £20 on the person to most effectively use that £100. In my experience many companies get this the wrong way around and 80% is spent on retraining, inspirational speakers, and the like.

Indeed, Sidney Decker, in his hugely influential "Field Guide to Understanding Human Error" would argue that my "at least 80%" is actually an underestimate and says bluntly:-

"human error is not the cause but the effect. Whatever the label (loss of situational awareness, inadequate resources, (even) complacency) human error can never be the conclusion of your investigation. It is the starting point".

That's worth restating:- the efficiency of your response and any use of organisational resource has an upper limit set by the accuracy of your analysis. A couple of quotes from all time greats:-

"A problem is that if you solved a problem effectively yesterday with a hammer then tomorrow everything is going to look like a nail" (James Reason)

"Always walk for a mile in a man's shoes before you judge them" (Elvis)

Just Culture

You'll find if you analyse objectively that many unsafe behaviours are out and out *unintentional* errors caused by design, task demands, ergonomics or lack of training. (I don't know what I'm doing and/or I'm physically or mentally incapable of doing it – especially if I'm tired!). Further, many conscious **violations** (a deliberate breaking of the rules) are often caused by the need to get finished before midnight and encouraged with 'blind eye' syndrome! (If this weren't the case then 'work to rule' wouldn't be such an effective strategy). So, often, an unsafe act is undertaken because the person feels that was what the company wanted. For example, we do a job well one week and cut a few corners but though this is known the only feedback given is "good job , well done" and you guarantee the same corners will be cut again next week. If you wanted to be emotive about it you could almost call this "grooming".

In the first section we detailed what a 'mindful' organisation looks like. In doing so we covered dozens of day-to-day events that cue the workforce to a view of what management "really, really want" that is a long way from world class safety.

The core of a 'Just Culture' then is to step back and apply some objective analysis before rushing to judgement. Just asking "why?" in a genuinely *'curious'* manner will pretty much do it. If you do you'll find that in 80 to 90% of cases you'll learn something interesting even if it's just that there's a systemic **temptation** to cut a corner.

This 'Just Culture' approach simply has to involve talking with and listening to the workforce if it is to be done at all well. It has an added benefit too. Research shows clearly that the more 'Just' a culture is perceived to be then the more effective the basic incident reporting and analysis system because there it maximises objectivity in analysis and more openness in reporting. It also impacts well on claims, turnover, absenteeism, motivation …

I'd like to argue strongly therefore that talking about transformational safety leadership without explicit reference to Just Culture and "Why?" analysis is, to me really missing a trick. We need thorough planning and analysis too. Willie John McBride (who led the aforementioned Lions to success in South Africa in 1974) might have been the most inspirational rugby captain ever but the coaching the squad received in preparation is now acknowledged as truly groundbreaking.

To address the basic analytical **methodologies** of a Just Culture:-

The 'Curious Why?'

If a company can double the number of times managers ask the question "why?" *curiously* – and, of course, do something with the answers - then the safety culture will be transformed. I guarantee it.

Importantly, it's worth stressing, the "why?" question **must** be asked with a **curious** tone. Asked aggressively the person will very likely get defensive and clam up.

Even if the answer is that it *is* the person in question you still learn something. (In this case that the person you're talking to is "bang to rights" and a more *robust* response is appropriate. That would be the *justice* in "Just Culture" perhaps!) The good news is that by being systematically analytical first any such "justice" is both less frequent and transparently **fairer** when it does happen. This in itself helps move the whole company culture forward.

As intimated above of course the trick is to then do something with all this learning ... and of course many organisations find this very difficult.

At the IOSH rail conference 2011 East Midland's trains produced some graphs showing impressive improvements and made the comment:-

> *"For us the key was to stop treating SPADs (signals passed at danger) as events in themselves but as symptoms of a more underlying issue. That shift in mindset was vital..."*

The Hypothetical "Anything Slow or Uncomfortable?" Question

If no issues have been raised by the initial discussion or observation then the person running the safety contact needs to lead a hypothetical discussion of issues that might arise.

It's even easier to transform a safety culture by doubling the number of times a manager asks the hypothetical "anything slow or uncomfortable?" question because in most companies it's simply not happening *at all.*

Almost half the Westminster MPs had to pay back expenses having given in to the temptation of over egging expense claims – a small percentage getting themselves into serious trouble. (Interestingly, many new MPs who resisted initially gave testimony they came under pressure from the old hands not to "make them look bad" a classic example of the pervasiveness of existing culture – but that's another book!). It's also said that the financial crisis of 2008 was triggered by the abundance of cheap credit available in the years leading up to it. To quote Michael Lewis in the Sunday Times:-

> *"The tidal wave of cheap money that rolled across the planet between 2002 and 2007 wasn't just money it was **temptation**. It offered entire societies the chance to reveal aspects of themselves they could not normally afford to indulge. Entire*

countries were told "the lights are out you can do whatever you want in the dark... " Americans wanted to own homes far larger than they could afford, Icelanders wanted to stop fishing and become investment bankers and the Greeks wanted be treated as a properly functioning northern European economy but whilst carrying on as normal with an inefficient and corrupt culture but one that was now in the Eurozone so with access to cheap and secure loans".

All married premiership footballers can sleep around at will. From reading the papers I suspect that like the expense grabbing politicians almost half of them do since the "getting into serious trouble" percentage itself is so high!

What the MPs, footballers and whole countries behaviour demonstrates (yet again) is that faced with a temptation very many people will give in to it and Stephen Fry says that when faced with a temptation he "gives in to it straight away to save on the faffing about".

ABC analysis (a technique described in more depth in my ASM book and others) shows us that even where the long term consequences of behaviour can be very important it's the short term consequences of that behaviour that often determine whether it happens or not. ABC stands for *antecedents, behaviours and consequences* – with antecedents meaning all triggers - such as training and signage - and anything contextual that's relevant – such as the fact that the person is tired.

So, for example, we smoke and drink and eat rich food and skip the gym and hope for the best regarding such illnesses as heart disease and cancer and we speed in our cars to save time though we know driving is by far the most dangerous thing we'll ever do.

This principle is important in work as when the safe way is slow, uncomfortable or inconvenient, we are tempted to cut the corner and "crack on". And of course we nearly always get away with it which is nice and rewarding and validates our instinctive "dynamic risk assessment". However, the laws of Heinrich's Triangle tell us that inevitably one of the corner cutters will cop for it sooner or later.

Therefore, I'd argue that where there is a temptation to cut a corner because the safe way is slow or inconvenient in some way it's as systemic a risk as an unguarded drop or piece of machinery. Because, as above, people are people and not robots, unsafe behaviour in these circumstances is almost **inevitable** for many and it's just a question of how soon someone gets hurt.

We can therefore wait until an incident and find out about these temptations from a (good) accident investigation. (Then we can exhort our workers not to give in to such temptations – a thankless task). Or we can pro-actively get out and about and discover these temptations and whenever practicable, *design them out.*

Using the Information

As with a "why" analysis any suggestion received that is agreed to be "high impact: low cost" should be invested in as soon as possible. In addition, the people who came up with the analysis should be lavished with praise both personally and through such media as newsletters. In the language of the "One Minute Manager" praising safe behaviour or "catching someone doing something right" is often argued to be a magic bullet all of its own but I'm assuming that's something readers will already know about.

We are very good at spotting mistakes – it's hot wired into us as people – but we are less good at spotting safe behaviour. Consider the contents of *any* newspaper or TV news programme and how you'd feel if someone asked to "talk to you about your behaviour". Blame comes naturally to us – for example how much of your last "good old gossip" was positive? We need to develop techniques that embed 'praising' as a habit.

However, I'd argue that even more motivating than praise is listening to someone and then acting on anything sensible they say. If, as Oscar Wilde said, "imitation is the sincerest form of flattery" then actually going away and putting someone's knowledge and experience into *action* is as sincere as praise can get. As mentioned above, in the "Undercover Boss" half the workers told "I'm going to use that" actually welled up.

Some Quick "How Well Do We Do This" Audit Questions. Ask the workforce if they've been asked recently "Is there's anything slow or inconvenient about doing the job safely"? Often you'll find the answer is *never* and so obviously some ABC analysis training should be rolled out. Another interesting question is "Could you make doing this job safely more convenient or comfortable?" If the answer is yes then, again, it's vital to investigate if that knowledge can be turned into a cost effective solution.

At a more basic level you might also ask them when they were last praised for a safe behaviour. If they respond by laughing you might like to roll out some "how to give feedback" training.

As a reminder of the points above here's a checklist of questions the answers to which might really help you understand what's really going on:-

- Why did you do that? (Why asked *curiously*)
- Is there anything slow, uncomfortable or inconvenient about doing this job safely?
- Do they genuinely have the time to do it safely? (The basic "is it an error or a violation"? question is "*can* they do it safely?" and to distinguish an optimising/ situational violation from an individual one "*realistically*, can they do it safely without inconvenience or discomfort?"

Other questions worth asking yourself (or the person being talked to if they trust you enough to answer):-

- How often does this unsafe act occur?
- How many do it?
- Has it ever been seen by a supervisor – what did they do when they saw it?
- What did they do when they saw it done safely? and
- What do peers say if they see it?

I should also of course refer the reader back to the list of questions at the end of the introductory chapter where, at the end of the section on the 'mindful' organisation, we list a couple of dozen key issues **always** worth investigating.

Summary of Key Points

• An unasked "curious why" question is a learning opportunity missed because you need to be discussing solutions at a root cause level not at a symptom level.

• If the safe way is slow, inconvenient or uncomfortable in any way then the bottom of Heinrich's Triangle will be filling up quickly. Pro-actively seek out if this is so...

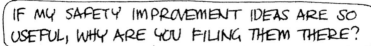

2.3 Coaching

This element of the safety contact is all about the 'inspirational' leadership behaviours we discussed at the start of the book. It's often said that the worst way to get a person to do something is to tell them to do it and this is certainly this is true of the typical western worker. We are a contrary and complicated lot are we not? (Please insert your own stories here!)

Developing a good style is important here as if we are threatening or annoying they'll not be working **with** us when we want to consider "what if?" scenarios, they'll be thinking "who the hell are you ...?". So we need to introduce ourselves, break the ice, put them at their ease and avoid confrontation if at all possible.

Even if the person we're talking to is provocative or incorrect we shouldn't take them on and/or "put them right" (unless that's unavoidable and/or appropriate) we should instead use techniques like the flat bat neutral paraphrase to confirm we're listening even if not necessarily agreeing. For example, "so what you're saying is all management are paper pushing big girl's blouses who haven't done a day's proper work in their lives ... ok, well that's a view and you obviously feel passionately about it – but please could you put down the hammer and tell me how you think we could improve our performance?"

On the other hand, if we decide to do something then there's no stopping us. In the original book we discussed the famous phenomenon of the Scottish football fans who began behaving well at foreign tournaments after being praised for their good natured party with Brazilian fans after a narrow but rather glorious defeat in a world cup. The headlines were "Scots in big party with Brazilians after heroic exit – hardly any arrests. What a contrast with the English!" Ever since then Scottish fans have made an effort to show up the English. With the Rangers fans behaviour in Manchester a few years ago being an exception to prove a rule. (The council, aware of this reputation were accused of assuming that all would be well and that they didn't need to make proper provision).

As well as being much more likely to induce light bulb "oh I see!" learning adopting a coaching style is important because we want the person to learn to risk assess automatically. We need them to get into the habit of asking "what if?" questions. Behavioural scientists stress that the future is more emotionally arousing precisely because it hasn't happened yet. There's the added emotion of uncertainty (who's not more scared when it's dark?) but also the energising possibility of **control**. Therefore, discussing the **future** is sewing fertile mental soil if you like.

This section looks at some basic techniques for ensuring the coaching element of the safety talk go well and this whole section is about encouraging the workforce to be active rather than passive in their thinking and behaviour.

The Feedback Fish – Coaching Basics

In the UK many supervisors need to be taught techniques for doing this at all naturally but if you understand the principle of the "feedback fish" you'll understand the basics of coaching. Imagine your five year old has brought you a picture of a fish and it's pretty rubbish - just a rough outline with no detail. You wouldn't say "that's crap that!" you'd first compliment it's brilliance and then hint about things that would improve it by asking "let me think – how do fish see?" and the five year old will shout "eyes!" and draw one in.

Though the fish is a simple, even childish, example the analogy is actually strong. Studies show that for ownership to kick in, the key thing seems to be that the person being coached is the one that *says the answer first out loud*, even if both people talking know full well that the 'coach' knew the answer and led them to it with questions.

Of course, like everything else in this section, using questioning technique rather than telling is a key component of good leadership *generally*. Indeed the major principles are all totally generic of course with *all* the most powerful coaching techniques having just as direct a relevance for safety

Ownership and Involvement

The quality guru Deming said that "you most own what you helped create".

To a busy manager ownership and involvement can look very similar at a glance but in practise they aren't at all. *Involvement* is asking the usual suspects to ratify or comment on a decision already provisionally taken by management. A better version of involvement is having them part of the team that takes the decision but it will almost certainly involve the usual suspects still. *Ownership* is giving the workforce itself a blank piece of paper and asking "what do you think?" (I've heard several quality gurus make the assertion that "since you'll work 3 times harder on your idea than on mine, mine needs to be 4 times better than yours before I'll impose it in you!")

Inevitably, where the workforce has a good level of ownership of safety the safety culture will be strong. I don't think I've ever seen a single example that contradicts this.

I think involvement and ownership is like the scrum in the middle of a rugby pitch. From the stands, whether the scrum is inching forwards or backwards it looks much the same - but if you're the No8 or scrum half on the pitch who has to do something with the ball it can make all the difference in the world.

Rewarding (Praise)

Obviously the use of praise is a key chapter in *any* text on good leadership, coaching or empowerment. This short section looks not so much at getting your supervisors to do it well but at getting them to do it *at all*!

Many people will have heard of the 'one minute manager' whose golden rule was "catch someone doing something right" and there are any number of classic texts that stress its importance in maximising your organisation's potential. Indeed studies suggest that praise is something like 20 times as effective in changing a person's behaviour as criticism. So as well as being more pleasant and the spin off benefits that go along with it think of all the time it can save! Studies also show that in order for criticism to resonate and not be seen as yet another nag it needs to have been preceded by five praises. These ratios might be arguable but the principle is sound. Praise is much more effective than criticism and greatly underused.

An interesting spot check is to ask a workforce how many instances of praise they get relative to criticism. It isn't ever 1 to 5 that's for sure! Indeed when doing our culture surveys we have a scale that ranges from "derisory laughter" all the way through to "no, that's not true - *never* isn't fair - I was praised once last year I think!" (I exaggerate but not by much).

Now, some US "how to praise" videos are a deep joy to watch and the more hard bitten and world weary the supervisors watching it, the more amusing!

> *"Hey Joe, I just wanna say how great it is to see you in all your PPE there ... you won't be the one going home missing an eye tonight ... so way to go Joe!"*

And cue Eric Morecombe giving a half turn and into his sleeve the muffled shout of *"Arsenal!!"* Or something like that!

"One in Ten". There are, however, more UK friendly techniques out there and one we use is stolen directly from educational psychologists and is called the "One in Ten" technique.

This technique is to ask someone to rate themselves on a task 1 to 10 and then (when they say 7 perhaps) not ask "why only a 7!?" but instead "why aren't you a 0?" Then, when they explain why they justify a 7 you listen, nod, smile, murmur and maybe even say "sounds more like an 8 to me!" But then with some rapport built and some praise naturally given for what they actually do well you switch to coaching mode asking:-

"but you know I'm a safety coach and my job is top halve accidents around here so if I can get you up from that 8 to a 9 that's my job done – well for now at least - how do you think we could do that?"

I'm sure you can imagine the two people are now well primed to have a productive and constructive chat from here. This especially as it nearly always leads naturally to "curious why?" questions and the other objective analysis techniques that we keep stressing as vital. Importantly it works well even in the UK and other European countries. A few weeks ago a Head of Safety of a company using the approach told me:-

"The other day I walked past a real old school head banger ... and he was actually having a constructive safety chat with one of our team. I tell you I thought well I'll be *&^%!!" (You'll forgive me if I take that as perhaps some of the best praise I've ever received).

Since this chap runs a ship yard in Portsmouth I'll argue if they can use it well *anyone* can. (Indeed, it transpired that their 11 safety reps undertaking 3 "1 in 10" talks a week was their **entire** Behavioural Safety process. I asked them if that worked for them and talked them through the 5 steps here... they said "but all the other "why?" stuff flows naturally from that anyway ...")

The important point I think though is that one of the problems we face constantly is that we're asked to do something that is sensible and effective but because it comes straight from a textbook (or a HQ in another country like the US) it isn't *appropriate* in Europe in its original format and goes down like a lead balloon.

Staying with the US, a good example of inspirational leadership is perhaps the most famous speech of them all, Dr Martin Luther King's 'I have a dream'. It's an excellent example of flexibility. The key words we all remember weren't actually in the formal draft and his speech was a bit leaden apparently until an aide tapped his arm and whispered "Why not try that 'dream' stuff that went down so well in the church the other day?"

So some lessons on *listening* to the people around us in there too!

Therefore I'd like to argue that there's an important generic lesson from the shipyard example and it's that we mustn't give up on a sound but rather tricky principle – praise in this case - just because of early setbacks. We must be flexible and persistent and find a better, more appropriate way of applying it locally.

Listening

Listening is key for two reasons. One, because you might learn something (as under 'analysis' above) but two, because it also helps empower the person you're listening too. Here I'd like to quote perhaps the most revered modern leader of them all.

When locked up on Robin Island Nelson Mandela would make a point of spending as much time as possible talking to his guards. Not just because he was trying to convert South Africa one person at a time - though he was of course - but because:-

"In genuinely listening to them I learned so much about the Boar mindset. Their values, hopes and fears. It stood me in such good stead later when we opened formal negotiations. I had more understanding and more respect".

It informed his decision to get behind the previously hated Springboks in the 1995 rugby world cup and not to force through a change of jersey as the ANC had voted to do. It led to one of the most unifying events in world history as depicted in the film "Invictus". (Morgan Freeman even won an Oscar)! And to address the second point directly – that you can influence the person you listen to by the very act of listening – we all know just how many of these guards were later in attendance at his presidential inauguration shedding tears of joy.

The Use of "Rational Data" – Perhaps the Best Coaching Technique Saved Until Last?

Research suggests that the single best way of changing a person's behaviour is through the use of *rational data*. Ideally, this will be backed up with some memorable *illustration*. For example, about half of all LTIs in the offshore industry are caused by falling down the stairs at a cost of tens of millions of pounds to the industry but the likelihood of a fall being only 100,000 to 1 (or some such). This means that if a person who never holds the handrail gets lucky they might go an entire career without falling – and a supervisor has a good excuse for not making a challenge. After all a fall is unlikely on any given day and they may face some scorn or even abuse from the person they challenge.

COACHING

However, imagine a person trying this:-

> *"I've just been on a course about behavioural safety and did you know that 50% of all LTIs out here are falling down the stairs... costs the industry about £12m annually... wonder how many jobs that is in the day and age?"*

Pause ...

> *"Only I noticed you weren't ..."*

I'm sure you can imagine a conversation would be much more likely to go well from here. The reason is simple – absolutely *no one* likes to be wrong but most of us are happy to admit that we don't know everything and are comfortable about being "uninformed". (I did say *most!*)

On courses we like to ask how many people have recently challenged a taxi driver for not wearing his or her seat belt. It will be very few if any ... then we talk about how many people are killed by drivers who roll their cars and end up in the back seat. (It's always the diagonal seat they end up in – so though sitting directly behind the driver is perceived as rude it's much safer!). It's about 30,000 worldwide. Then we show an in-cab clip of a driver rolling his car and ending up in the back seat with some force. Even at 30mph (as in the clip) it makes for pretty spectacular viewing. Then we point out that at 60mph he'd go back with 4 times as much force...

Then we ask the audience if they'd be more likely to say something next time they get in a taxi and notice the driver is unbuckled... and nearly all hands go up.

A Personal Case Study in *Data* - "Micromorts". Just after the 2010 Christmas break I needed to visit a potential client in deepest Norfolk and chose to travel there by train. When discussing travel with the CEO he asked me why I'd not driven and I explained about 'micromorts'. A 'micromort', well worth looking up on Wikipedia, is basically a 1 in 1M chance of dying in an accident. (For example, it's every 6,000 miles in a train, 230 miles on a road, 6 on a motorbike; 180 yards on a motorbike if over the drink limit! And so on ...). I explained I'd been up late all holiday watching the cricket in Australia and the return to work was a bit of a shock. So that whilst the early part of the journey was OK (on a Motorway) the 4th or 5th hour of driving would have been at pub closing time, in the dark, on Norfolk's somewhat notorious "A" roads as fatigue set in. Though I'm not particularly risk averse I'd realised my micromort rating would go through the roof! (Note that the actual risk level remained pretty good – it was the dramatic ***increase*** in relative risk that made me wince a bit and reach for the train time-table).

He responded that many people had told him over the years they'd thought to get the train to them for similar reasons but hadn't. Except one chap - their advanced driver coach - who apparently *always* takes the train to them! So I like to think this is a good example of user friendly rational data helping you think like the pros! (And to square this whole "coaching" techniques circle entirely here. When this - at that time only *potential* - client said "Hmm ... I'm impressed to see that you walk the talk!" what do you think it did to my likelihood of doing it again next time?).

Quick 'How Well Do We Do This" Audit Questions.

• As with the above section we can simply ask a random sample of *typical* workers when they were last *genuinely* asked for their opinion and input regarding a safety issue.

• We can ask them when they were last asked to consider "what if?"

• We can ask when they were last praised for a safe act.

• We can ask when the last time someone explained "why" to them in a way that made logical sense because they used data and illustration – whether it be about a change, a rule or some such.

Summary of Key Points

• Praise is many times more effective than criticism
• Discussing "what if?" about the future is much more energising than discussing the past.
• Use questions to draw out knowledge and gain 'buy-in'. It really doesn't matter if you lead them to an answer – so long as they say it first!
• Rational data and illustration is the most effective way to change someone
• Remember that "a person most owns what they helped create"

AS HIS COLLEAGUES COULD TESTIFY, BOB'S COACHING STYLE LEFT A LOT TO BE DESIRED

2.4 Eliciting a Promise?

A very short chapter this one!

If the above techniques are done well then this will take care of itself *and you won't need to address it directly at all*. And anyway a promise that doesn't come from within spontaneously probably isn't worth having. So, if you do get a spontaneous promise then simply thank them for it with as much warmth as you can.

That said there will be times when - if nothing else - the *law* obligates you to point something out and get a promise not to repeat. Another example would be where a solution is "high impact but high cost" and not likely to be addressed any time soon, if at all. If this is the case a little bit of psychology can help.

The Eyes and "I's" Have It

Studies have found that if a person looks you in the eyes and uses the "I" word when making a promise they are something like 3 times less likely to go on to break that promise. You don't want them looking at the ground and mumbling "sure, no problem … I'm on it" or some such. That's just a grown up version of crossing your fingers behind your back!

For example, imagine you're on a beach and a complete stranger asks you to look after their kit for 5 minutes whilst they get their kids an ice cream or some such. If you look at them and say "I will" how long will you stay? If they never come back would you bundle the stuff up and leave a note? It's because an internal "integrity" switch is subconsciously switched on when you (as my children say) "pinky promise".

To look at this from the other side how confident would you feel about leaving your kit with someone who avoids your eyes and mumbles "sure" in the general direction of the sea?

So when it comes to promises the "Eyes" and the "I's" really do have it.

Summary of Key Point

- A vague promise made to the floor is 3 times as likely to be broken as an "I" promised made looking you in the eye. If you need a promise make sure it's a *promise*, promise!

BOB'S ATTEMPTS AT SINCERE PRAISE WERE STILL
CONSIDERED A LITTLE OVER THE TOP IN THE FOUNDRY

2.5 Close Out

As ever, follow up is perhaps the most important section of all because if you get this one wrong much of what was right above will be undone. There are really only a few things to remember here...

The first is to say thank you for anything at all sensible that comes out of the discussion. And thank them warmly and sincerely too. Remember that 85% of a communication isn't in what we say it's about *how* we say it. If you're going through the motions they'll know.

You might even like to use Bill Clinton's trick of making some sort of physical touch to add emphasis. Apparently how sincere he was trying to be followed this line:-

• Warm hand shake
• Warm hand shake with left hand clasped over joined hands
• Warm hand shake with left hand clasped about forearm
• Warm hand shake with left hand clasped on shoulder

Some commentators said it correlated with how big the lie he was telling but that's sheer cynicism! I'm sure you get the point! Whether he was lying or not – and you may be shocked to know that apparently sometimes he was - it worked very well for Bill! In the UK just a sincere handshake and smile should suffice.

The Learning Requires A Plan of Action?

Ideally any agreements here will be SMART

• Specific;
• Measurable;
• Agreed;
• Realistic
• Time set.

Obviously, the second thing is that if you get a high impact low cost solution to a problem – implement it! Or arrange for it to be implemented, if more appropriate, and follow up with the person you delegated to with a "Did you sort out X and did you get back to Y afterwards to let them know how it turned out?!" Unless it's all affirmative don't let it go. Demonstrate your genuine commitment by your persistence.

CLOSE OUT

Then let the person know what you've done and say thank you (again). Then get their picture in an in-house magazine… (or some such!)

The third thing is even simpler to describe but harder to do. If you say you'll follow something up and let them know how it goes then you have to do so. Even a simple "it seems it's a lot more complicated when you get into it than it looks", is better than sweet … well than **nothing**.

2.5.1 A Suggestion - A Person Whose Job is to Cover All the Weaknesses

As we've made clear several times above, knowledge itself - like a great check-sheet - is no use at all if we don't use it and feedback and communication is key. We really don't care how a company does the things above or who does it – in good behavioural tradition we just care that it gets done, gets done well and gets done quickly. That said we'd like to suggest a role that can be done part time (or even full time in a big company) that directly address the several major weaknesses we often see.

We'd recommend that some of the workforce be trained up as behavioural safety/human error champions. Basically, they'll need to understand the basics of human error and this will require a few days of training. They will also need a senior manager mentor who can clear blockages and write cheques. Then their task is to:-

- be the first point of call for any ideas and suggestions that come out of a safety contact (to make it easy for the supervisor or manager)
- be the first point of call for any worker who has an idea – maybe just after a safety contact has taken place (or at any other time).
- tell people what's happening and why. Not just verbally but via notice-boards all can see …
- get back to anyone who was part of putting something in the system to let them know what's happening or at least explaining why if nothing seems to be happening.
- be consulted whenever a change occurs – even if the change is not anticipated to have a safety impact!
- look at the hiring process from a safety perspective
- look at supplier selection and contracting
- be involved in the purchasing of equipment …

And also:-

- Running or at least helping with the on-going process safety audits …

You might like to think of them as the "sweeper of unintended consequences" as discussed towards the end of section one.

It's a simple idea. They simply take the inconvenience out of the above process whenever possible to bridge the gap between good intentions and actions. Again, as mentioned above pro-actively designing out inconvenience is always a good idea. They also keep the information and feedback loops up to speed …

Summary of Key Point

"The road to hell is paved with good *intentions*"

3 Conclusion

Boiled down these safety visits are pretty simple. What we're trying to do is to communicate clearly the standards we'd like and throw an appropriate leadership shadow to inspire safer behaviour by setting an example, empowering and coaching. We're trying to learn why things aren't perfect and to show our *genuine* commitment by doing something with that learning whenever that's financially or logistically viable.

At the start of the booklet I suggested that we get the safety and health standards we are prepared to accept and that we communicate this with our leadership over and above compliance and process integrity.

By being out there talking about safety and using the information and learning we demonstrate our commitment. By leading properly we inspire "willing followers" and by working from a 'Just Culture' perspective we enhance trust and fairness and learn how best to use our scarce resources.

It's very much easier said than done of course – but it really isn't rocket science.

Checklist.

The following questions are provided as a simple reminder of the key points. If you are able to answer yes to the majority of them after a safety conversation then I *guarantee* you'll have laid another brick in the wall of a strong safety culture.

1 Were you able to get the person talking to you in a reasonably relaxed and natural way?

2 Did the conversation remain professional and focused and not overly "matey"

3 Did you ask "why?" *curiously* about any issues seen or raised?

4 Did you pro-actively ask "anything slow, uncomfortable or inconvenient?" about doing your job safely

5 We're you able to praise something you saw. Or praise came naturally because you used a technique like the "rate yourself 1 to 10" approach.

6 Did you use a questioning coaching technique to get them to be the one to come up with any answer?

7 Were any promises made to you inclusive of the "I" word whilst looking you in the eyes?

8 We're any actions agreed SMART?

Finally,

9 Do you acknowledge that whether we're talking about SMART actions you've committed to do yourself, actions delegated that need following up - or just getting out there and undertaking a safety talk at all. RUDE NIKE RULES ALWAYS APPLY?!

References:-

A Daniels and J. Agnew "Safe By Accident?" Performance Management Publications, 2010

S Dekker "The Field Guide to Understanding Human Error", Ashgate 2006

E. S. Geller "The Psychology of Safety Handbook", Lewis Publishing, 2001

N. J. Goldstein, S. J. Martin and R. B. Cialdini "Yes! 50 Secrets of Persuasion" Profile Books, 2007

A Hopkins, "Failure to Learn" CCH Australia, 2008

N Mandella, "Long Walk to Freedom", Abacus, 1994

J Reason, "Managing the Risks of Organisational Accidents", Ashgate, 1997 and "The Human Contribution", Ashgate, 2008.

R.H Thaler and C.R. Sunstein, "Nudge", Penguin, 2009

If you find the material in this book interesting can I strongly recommend the following very readable books – for a long journey or perhaps as the non fiction one for a holiday!:-

D. Brown "Tricks of the Mind" 4 Books, 2007

M Gladwell, "Blink" and "The Tipping Point" Penguin, 2005

J. T. Hallinan "Why We Make Mistakes" Broadway Books, 2009

S Levitt and S Dunbar "Freakonomics" and "Superfreakonomics" Penguin, 2009

B. Mc Farlan, "Drop the Pink Elephant" Capstone, 2004